KIM SCHAEFER

Flowering Quilts

16 CHARMING FOLK ART PROJECTS TO DECORATE YOUR HOME

C&T PUBLISHING

Text © 2006 Kim Schaefer

Artwork © 2006 C&T Publishing, Inc.

Publisher: Amy Marson

Editorial Director: Gailen Runge

Acquisitions Editor: Jan Grigsby

Editor: Liz Aneloski

Technical Editors: Helen Frost, Wendy Mathson

Copyeditor/Proofreader: Wordfirm, Inc.

Cover Designer: Kristen Yenche

Design Director/Book Designer: Kristen Yenche

Illustrator: Richard Sheppard

Production Assistant: Kirstie L. Pettersen

Photography: Luke Mulks, unless otherwise noted

Published by C&T Publishing, Inc., P.O. Box 1456, Lafayette, CA 94549

Front cover: Star Flowers Wall Quilt

Back cover: Big Happy Flowers Table Runner, Garden Path Lap Quilt

Schaefer, Kim

 Flowering quilts : 16 charming folk art projects to decorate your home / Kim Schaefer.

   p. cm.

 ISBN 1-57120-338-9 (paper trade)

1. Quilting—Patterns. 2. Patchwork—Patterns. 3. Flowers in art. I. Title.

 TT835.S284 2006

 746.46'041—dc22

 2005017589

Printed in China

10 9 8 7 6 5 4 3 2 1

Dedication

To all quilters, past, present, and future.

Acknowledgments

Thanks to the following individuals:

My husband, Gary Schaefer, who has given me continued support and encouragement in everything I've done. He believed in me and pushed me to take risks I never would have taken without him. Most of all, I thank him for letting me do all the fun things in life while he works out the technical difficulties.

My sons, Max, Ben, Sam, and Gator, for all the time they were ignored and told to go away and be quiet, and for becoming uncomplaining connoisseurs of frozen pizza, Hamburger Helper, and Ramen soup while I worked on this book.

My mom, Alice Sanders, who took pity on her grandsons and cooked for them.

My daughter Cody, for her humor and enthusiasm.

My daughter Ali, for her thoughtful gift of earplugs to decrease the volume of the "Neanderthals" and for her command of the English language.

My mom again, and my dad, Jerry Sanders, for their unwavering support and encouragement and for instilling in me the belief and confidence that I could do anything I wanted with hard work and perseverance.

Lynn Helmke, longarm quilter extraordinaire, whose creativity and expertise enhanced all the quilts in this book.

Trudie Hughes, a gifted and competent teacher who has inspired me and hundreds of other students with her enthusiasm and technical know-how.

I chose C&T to publish this book because they are, quite simply, the best. I would like to thank the entire C&T staff for their patience and professionalism.

Special thanks to editor Liz Aneloski, technical editor Helen Frost for her hard work in checking the accuracy of all the patterns and for being so easy to work with, Richard Sheppard for the fine illustrations, and Kristen Yenche for the great cover and book design.

Contents

Introduction 3

General Instructions 4

Potted Flowers Table Runner 6

Big Happy Flowers Table Runner 10

Checkerboard Tulip Table Runner 14

Sunflower Table Runner 18

Star Flowers Wall Quilt 21

Log Cabin Pot Wall Quilt 24

Raggy Flowers Wall Quilt 27

A Bloomin' Dozen Wall Quilt 32

Folksy Flower Vases Wall Quilt 40

Raggy Flowers Lap Quilt 47

Stripes and Flower Vines Lap Quilt 50

Square Flowers Lap Quilt 55

Red-Eyed Blooms Lap Quilt 59

Garden Path Lap Quilt 63

Pocketful of Posies Quilt 70

Red Posies Quilt 74

About the Author 79

 # Introduction

This book presents a collection of scrappy, folksy, floral quilts that combine traditional piecing techniques with machine appliqué. You will find a variety of projects, including table runners, wall quilts, lap quilts, and large quilts. The projects range in difficulty from very easy to intermediate level.

Scrap quilts have been among the best loved and most used quilts throughout history. They appeal to both the eye and the heart. Collecting the fabric used in scrap quilts is a labor of love (my husband says compulsion). As quilters, we seem to accumulate fabric pieces, and most of us have a good stash to choose from. Mr. Webster defines *stash* as "to put by or away as for safe keeping for future use, usually in a secret place." I believe Mr. Webster would have made a fine quilter. A scrap quilt provides a great opportunity to utilize your stash. All the projects in this book are basically scrappy, with some occasional cheating; if I don't have it, I go to the quilt shop and buy it.

I want to say a few words about appliqué. Let me say first that I truly love and appreciate traditional hand appliqué and the time and workmanship that goes into making a gorgeous hand-appliquéd quilt. I made one. I will probably never make another. Machine appliqué is a great alternative. I love what machine appliqué offers: a timesaving technique capable of producing beautiful results. If you are a busy quilter, try machine appliqué; you may never hand appliqué again.

General Instructions

ROTARY CUTTING

I cut all fabrics used in pieced blocks, borders, and bindings with a rotary cutter, acrylic ruler, and mat. I also trim blocks and borders with these tools.

PIECING

All piecing measurements include $\frac{1}{4}''$ seam allowances. If you sew an accurate $\frac{1}{4}''$ seam, you will have happiness, joy, and success in quilting. If you don't, you will have misery, tears, and the ripper.

There are many aspects of quilting that don't require perfection for a folk look: matching plaids, choosing fabrics in a scrap quilt, cutting the appliqué pieces. My biggest and best quiltmaking tip is to learn to sew a $\frac{1}{4}''$ seam.

PRESSING

Press seams to one side, preferably toward the darker color. Press flat and avoid sliding the iron over the pieces, as this can distort and stretch them. To join two seamed sections, press the seams in opposite directions. This makes it much easier to match seamlines and reduces bulk.

APPLIQUÉ

All appliqué instructions are for fusible web with machine appliqué. If you prefer a different appliqué method, you will need to add seam allowances to the appliqué pieces. Appliqué pieces have been drawn in reverse. A lightweight fusible web works best for machine appliqué. Choose your favorite and follow the manufacturer's directions.

1. Trace all parts of the appliqué design to the paper side of the fusible web. Trace each layer of the design separately. For example, all the petals on a flower are traced as one piece and the center as another. Add the pattern letter and/or number to each traced shape.

2. Cut loosely around the appliqué shapes, leaving a $\frac{1}{4}''$ margin around each piece.

3. Press and fuse the shapes to the *wrong* side of the fabric. Cut on the tracing lines and peel the paper backing off the appliqué web. A thin web will remain on the wrong side of the fabric, which will adhere the appliqué pieces to the backgrounds.

4. Position the pieces on the backgrounds. Press and fuse in place.

5. Machine stitch around the appliqué shapes using a zigzag, satin, or blanket stitch. Stitch any other lines on the patterns to add detail. A line of stitching defines the rim on the flower pots and the petals on some of the flowers.

My personal choice is the satin stitch. I use beige thread for all the stitching. Sometimes the stitches blend with the fabric and sometimes they don't. Using one color throughout gives the quilt a folk art look.

HALF-SQUARE TRIANGLES

Some of the projects use half-square triangle blocks (see *Star Flowers* on page 21). Because the quilts are scrappy I usually cut the triangles from squares and sew them individually. I always make more than I need so that I have choices when assembling the quilt top. In each project I will give the exact measurements used in that quilt. If you want to change the size of the blocks, it is important to know the basic formula for making half-square triangles. It is the finished size plus $\frac{7}{8}''$. If you need a 6″ finished block, cut the squares $6\frac{7}{8}'' \times 6\frac{7}{8}''$. Cut the squares in half diagonally once to make two triangles. I refer to this as "cut the square on the diagonal."

PUTTING IT ALL TOGETHER

When all the blocks are completed for a quilt, lay them out on the floor or, if you're lucky enough to have one, a design wall. Arrange and rearrange until you are happy with the overall look of the quilt. This is an especially important step in scrap quilting. Each project has specific directions for assembling the top. Refer to the diagrams and photos.

BORDERS

All borders in the book are straight cut, with no mitered corners. This renders a more folk look, and it's easier and faster too. Join strips together at a 45° angle, as necessary, to achieve the desired length.

LAYERING THE QUILT

Cut the batting and backing pieces 2″ to 3″ larger than the quilt top for runners and smaller quilts (less than 40″) and 3″ to 4″ larger than the quilt top for larger quilts. Lay the pressed backing on the bottom, with the right side facing down. Place the batting over the backing and the quilt top on top. Make sure everything is flat and smooth and the quilt top is centered over the batting and backing. Pin or baste the quilt.

QUILTING

How you quilt your top is a personal choice; you may prefer hand or machine quilting. My favorite is to send the quilt top to a longarm quilter. This method keeps my number of unfinished quilt tops low and finished quilts high.

COLOR AND FABRIC CHOICES

There are many books that cover color theory, addressing terms such as *analogous, secondary, complementary, primary, tonal value, color range,* and so on. In choosing fabric you will hear terms such as *scale, contrast, value,* and *balance.* I have a more relaxed approach to color and fabric choice. If I like it, I use it. Scrap quilting lends itself well to this approach. In general, the more fabrics I use, the more I like the quilt. Everyone has different tastes. In the end it's your quilt and your choice, and if you're happy, that's what's important.

MAKE THE QUILT YOUR OWN

It is my hope that you will use the projects in this book as inspiration and a starting point to make your own quilts. If you want to change the size of a quilt, simply add or subtract blocks or change the width of the borders. Feel free to enlarge or reduce the appliqué patterns at your local copy shop. Your color choices may be totally different from mine.

YARDAGE AND FABRIC REQUIREMENTS

Yardage and fabric requirements are given for each project, many calling for a "total" of assorted fabrics that can be used as a base for your quilt. The yardage amounts may vary depending on several factors: the size of quilt, the number of fabrics used, and the number of pieces you cut from each. Each yardage amount allows for one extra strip to be cut, in case of any cutting errors. I don't worry about running out of a particular fabric; for a scrappy look, this isn't a factor.

I prefer to use the lengthwise grain of the fabric for quilt backing, even on smaller projects. For larger quilts, I piece together two or three lengths of fabric.

Binding fabric amounts allow for 2″-wide strips cut on the straight of grain. Fusible web amounts are based on 17″ width.

Potted Flowers
Table Runner

S pread an array of potted flowers on your table. This runner goes together easily. Not long enough? Simply add more scrappy squares in the center. Not wide enough? Add more appliqué flower blocks.

Block Size: 4″ × 8″

Finished Table Runner: 18½″ × 38½″

MATERIALS

½ yard total of assorted lights for backgrounds

⅜ yard total of assorted golds, reds, and oranges for flowers

¼ yard total of assorted greens for stems and leaves

⅛ yard or scraps of rust for pots

¼ yard of light green for inner border

⅓ yard of dark green for outer border

1¼ yards for backing

⅓ yard for binding

½ yard of paper-backed fusible web

CUTTING

✽ Cut 24 squares 4½″ × 4½″ from lights for the background squares.

PIECED BACKGROUND

1. Sew 3 rows of 4 squares each for the center of the runner.

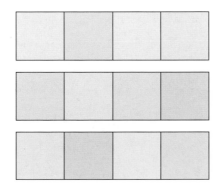

Piece center.

2. Sew together the 3 rows, forming a large rectangle.

APPLIQUÉ BLOCKS

1. Sew together 2 light 4½″ squares for appliqué block backgrounds. Make 6 sets.

2. Cut 6 each of patterns 1 and 2, reversing pattern 2 for blocks C, D, and F. Cut 1 each of the other patterns.

3. Appliqué the appropriate pieces onto each block.

Flower block A; make 1, finished size 4″ × 8″

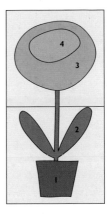

Flower block B; make 1, finished size 4″ × 8″

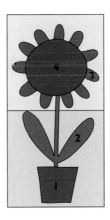

Flower block C; make 1, finished size 4″ × 8″

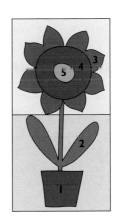

Flower block D; make 1, finished size 4″ × 8″

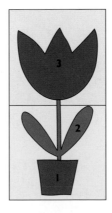

Flower block E; make 1, finished size 4″ × 8″

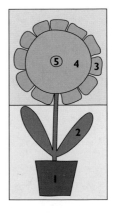

Flower block F; make 1, finished size 4″ × 8″

Putting It All Together

Referring to the quilt plan on this page and the color photo on page 6, sew the blocks together.

Borders

Inner Border

1. Cut 2 strips 1½″ × 32½″ for the side borders. Sew to the quilt top and press toward the border.

2. Cut 2 strips 1½″ × 14½″ for the top and bottom borders. Sew to the quilt top and press toward the border.

Outer Border

1. Cut 2 strips 2½″ × 34½″ for the side borders. Sew to the quilt top and press toward the border.

2. Cut 2 strips 2½″ × 18½″ for the top and bottom borders. Sew to the quilt top and press toward the border.

Finishing

1. Layer the runner top with batting and backing; baste or pin.

2. Quilt as desired and bind.

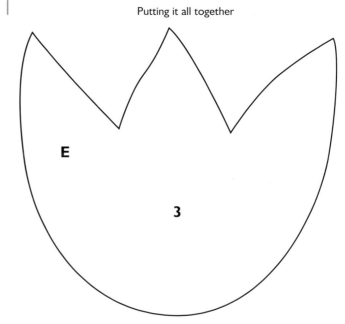

Putting it all together

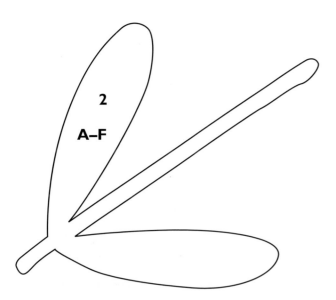

Big Happy Flowers
Table Runner

Brighten up your table with these big, bold, beautiful flowers. The size of the table runner may be altered by simply adding or removing blocks. It's sure to add sparkle to any décor. The flowers can be made all one color for a different look.

Block Size: 10″ × 10″

Finished Table Runner: 14½″ × 62½″

MATERIALS

⅓ yard each or scraps of 5 lights for appliqué block backgrounds

⅓ yard each or scraps of rust, purple, blue, red, and yellow for flowers

¼ yard each or scraps of rust, purple, blue, red, and yellow for flower centers

⅛ yard each or scraps of rust, purple, blue, red, and yellow for flower centers

½ yard total of assorted greens for pieced border

2 yards for backing

⅓ yard for binding

1½ yards of paper-backed fusible web

CUTTING

❀ Cut 5 squares 10½″ × 10½″ from light fabrics for the appliqué block backgrounds.

❀ Cut 92 squares 2½″ × 2½″ from assorted green scraps for the pieced border.

APPLIQUÉ BLOCKS

Cut 5 each of patterns 1, 2, and 3, rotating pattern 3 to complete the other half of the flower. Appliqué the appropriate pieces onto each block.

Appliqué block; make 5, finished size 10″ × 10″

PIECED BORDER

1. Sew 5 squares 2½″ × 2½″ to form a row. Make 4 sets for the pieced border between the appliqué blocks.

Make 4.

2. Sew the pieced border rows between the appliqué blocks. Refer to the diagram on page 12 and color photo on page 10.

3. Sew together a row of 29 squares 2½″ × 2½″ for the side borders. Make 2.

4. Sew together a row of 7 squares 2½″ × 2½″ for the top and bottom borders. Make 2.

PUTTING IT ALL TOGETHER

1. Refer to the quilt plan and sew the side borders to the table runner. Press toward the border. Sew the top and bottom borders. Press toward the border.

2. Layer the table runner with batting and backing; baste or pin.

3. Quilt as desired and bind.

Putting it all together

Alternate Color Option

Checkerboard Tulip
Table Runner

In Wisconsin, tulips are one of the first signs of a long-awaited spring. Brighten your kitchen with these potted beauties.

Appliqué Block Size: *6″ × 9″*

Finished Table Runner: *20½″ × 35½″*

MATERIALS

⅓ yard total of assorted lights for appliqué block backgrounds

¼ yard total of assorted lights for checkerboard backgrounds

¼ yard total of assorted reds for checkerboard backgrounds

¼ yard each or scraps of yellow, purple, rust, red, blue, and pink or scraps for tulips

⅛ yard or scraps of brown for pots

⅛ yard total of assorted greens for stems and leaves

⅛ yard or scraps of black for flower pistils

¼ yard of deep red for border

1⅛ yards for backing

⅓ yard for binding

⅝ yard of paper-backed fusible web

CUTTING

❀ Cut 15 squares 3½″ × 3½″ from red fabrics for the checkerboard backgrounds.

❀ Cut 15 squares 3½″ × 3½″ from light fabrics for the checkerboard backgrounds.

❀ Cut 6 rectangles 6½″ × 9½″ from light fabrics for the appliqué block backgrounds.

PIECED BACKGROUND

1. Sew 5 rows of 6 squares each for the center of the table runner.

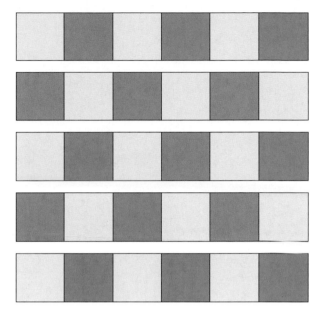

Piece center.

2. Sew together the 5 rows, forming a large rectangle.

APPLIQUÉ BLOCKS

Cut 6 each of patterns 1, 2, 3, 4, and 5. Appliqué the appropriate pieces onto each block.

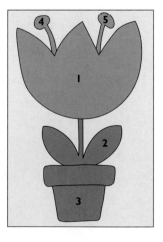

Flower block; make 6, finished size 6″ × 9″

PUTTING IT ALL TOGETHER

Referring to the quilt plan on this page and the color photo on page 14, sew the blocks together.

Border

1. Cut 2 strips 1½″ × 33½″ for the side borders. Sew to the quilt top and press toward the border.

2. Cut 2 strips 1½″ × 20½″ for the top and bottom borders. Sew to the quilt top and press toward the border.

Finishing

1. Layer the table runner top with batting and backing; baste or pin.

2. Quilt as desired and bind.

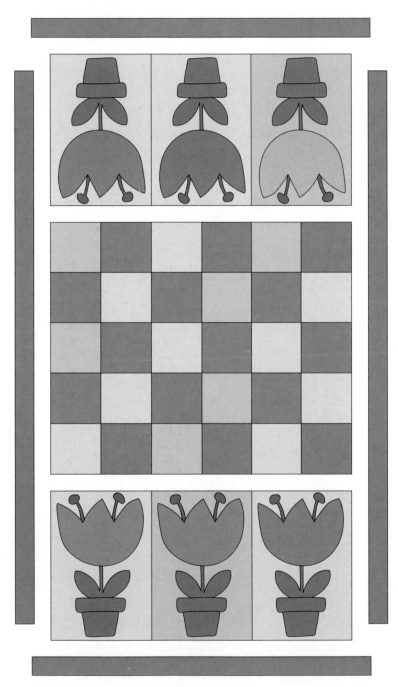

Putting it all together

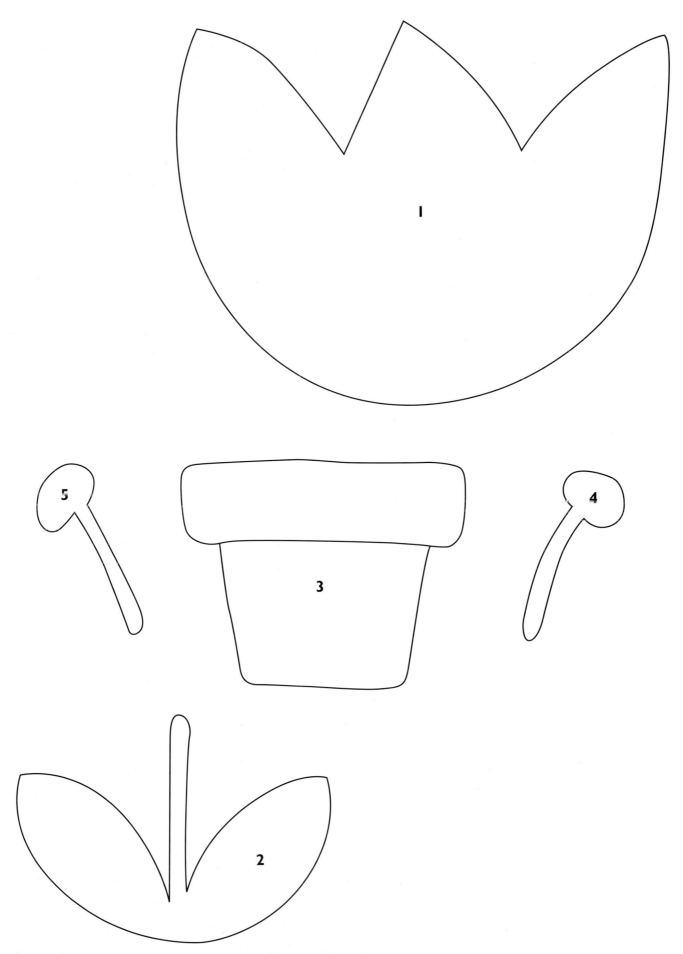

Sunflower
Table Runner

FLOWERING QUILTS

Big, bold, beautiful sunflowers spread warmth and charm. Celebrate the summer season with this simple table runner.

Block Size: 8″ × 8″

Finished Table Runner: 20½″ × 44½″

MATERIALS

⅓ yard or scraps of blue for appliqué block backgrounds

¼ yard each or scraps of 3 yellows for sunflowers

¼ yard each or scraps of 6 yellows and golds for flower centers

½ yard total of assorted yellows and golds for inner border

¾ yard total of assorted blues for outer border

1½ yards for backing

⅓ yard for binding

¾ yard of paper-backed fusible web

CUTTING

✿ Cut 3 squares 8½″ × 8½″ from blue for the appliqué block backgrounds.

✻ Cut 12 rectangles 2½″ × 4½″ from yellow and gold fabrics for the inner border.

✿ Cut 12 rectangles 2½″ × 6½″ from yellow and gold fabrics for the inner border.

✻ Cut 28 squares 4½″ × 4½″ from assorted blues for the outer border.

APPLIQUÉ BLOCKS

Cut 3 each of patterns 1, 2, and 3. Appliqué the appropriate pieces onto each block.

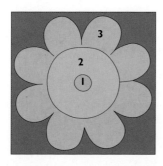

Sunflower block; make 3, finished size 8″ × 8″

PIECED BORDER

Inner Border

1. Sew together 2 rectangles 2½″ × 4½″ on the short ends. Make 6 sets for the inner borders.

2. Sew together 2 rectangles 2½″ × 6½″ on the short ends. Make 6 sets for the inner borders.

3. Referring to the quilt plan and the color photo, sew the inner borders to the appliqué blocks.

Outer Borders

1. Sew together 2 rows of 5 squares 4½″ × 4½″ for the top and bottom borders.

2. Sew together 2 rows of 9 squares 4½″ × 4½″ for the side borders.

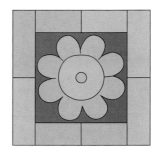

Piece inner borders.

PUTTING IT ALL TOGETHER

1. Referring to the quilt plan below and the color photo on page 18, sew the appliqué blocks and borders together. Press toward the inner border.

2. Layer the table runner with batting and backing; baste or pin.

3. Quilt as desired and bind.

Putting it all together

Alternate Color Option

FLOWERING QUILTS

Star Flowers
Wall Quilt

Star flowers will bloom all year in this wall quilt with folksy charm. Embellish the star flowers with your favorite buttons.

Block Size: 8″ × 8″

Finished Wall Quilt: 40½″ × 40½″

MATERIALS

¾ yard total of assorted lights for background triangles

1½ yards total of assorted blues, navies, reds, golds, oranges, rusts, purples, and greens for triangles, star flowers, stems, and leaves

¼ yard of red for inner border

½ yard of navy for outer border

2½ yards for backing

⅓ yard for binding

1¼ yards of paper-backed fusible web

16 of your favorite buttons

CUTTING

✿ Cut 32 squares 4⅞″ × 4⅞″ from assorted lights for the backgrounds.

✿ Cut the squares on the diagonal to yield 64 triangles.

Cut squares on diagonal.

✿ Cut 32 squares 4⅞″ × 4⅞″ from assorted darks for the backgrounds.

✿ Cut the squares on the diagonal to yield 64 triangles.

PIECED BACKGROUND

1. Sew the light triangles to the dark triangles on the diagonal edge.

Make 64.

2. Referring to the diagram below and the color photo on page 21, sew the background blocks.

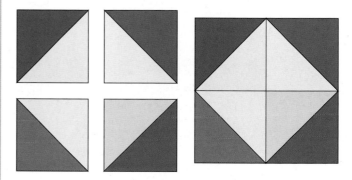

Make 16, finished size 8″ × 8″

APPLIQUÉ BLOCKS

Cut 16 each of patterns 1, 2, 3, 4, and 5. Appliqué the appropriate pieces onto each block.

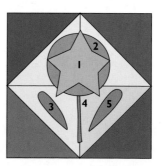

Star Flower block; make 16, finished size 8″ × 8″

PUTTING IT ALL TOGETHER

1. Referring to the quilt plan, sew together 4 rows of 4 blocks each.

2. Sew the rows together to form the quilt top.

Borders

Inner Border

1. Cut 2 strips 1½″ × 32½″ for the side borders. Sew to the quilt top and press toward the border.

2. Cut 2 strips 1½″ × 34½″ for the top and bottom borders. Sew to the quilt top and press toward the border.

Outer Border

1. Cut 2 strips 3½″ × 34½″ for the side borders. Sew to the quilt top and press toward the border.

2. Piece and cut 2 strips 3½″ × 40½″ for the top and bottom borders. Sew to the quilt top and press toward the border.

Finishing

1. Layer the quilt top with batting and backing; baste or pin.

2. Quilt as desired and bind.

3. Sew the buttons in the star centers, if desired.

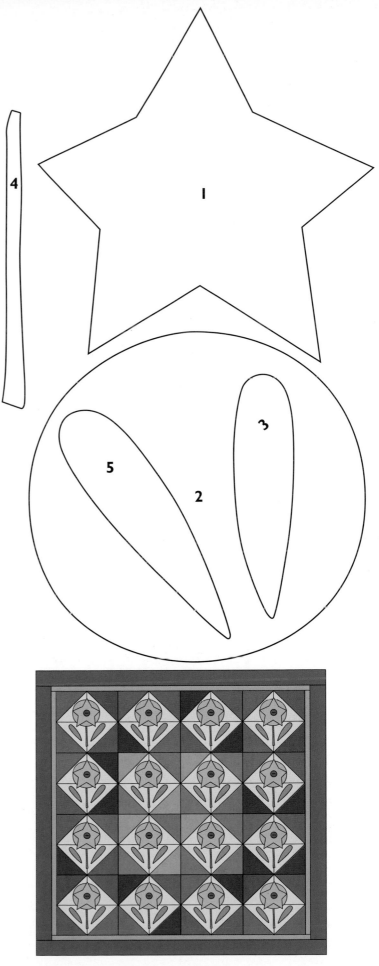

Putting it all together

Alternate Color Option

Log Cabin Pot Wall Quilt

Fun and folksy, this quilt will lend a whimsical touch to any room. The potted flowers are framed with a border of scrappy Courthouse Steps blocks (a variation of the Log Cabin block) and checkered side borders for a free-spirited folk art look.

Finished Wall Quilt: 40½″ × 40½″

MATERIALS

¾ yard of tan for appliqué background

¼ yard or scrap of rust for pot

¼ yard or scrap of gold for star

¼ yard each or scraps of rust, yellow, and red for flowers

⅛ yard each or scraps of 3 greens for stems and leaves

⅛ yard total of assorted reds for Log Cabin blocks

¾ yard total of assorted lights for Log Cabin blocks and checkered border

¾ yard total of assorted darks for Log Cabin blocks, checkered border, and flower centers

1¾ yards for backing and binding

¾ yard of paper-backed fusible web

CUTTING

❁ Cut 1 rectangle 21½″ × 19½″ from tan fabric for the appliqué block background.

Assorted reds
❁ Cut 6 rectangles 1½″ × 2″ for the center pieces.

Assorted lights
❁ Cut 6 rectangles 1½″ × 2″ for the Log Cabin blocks.

❁ Cut 6 rectangles 1½″ × 5″ for the Log Cabin blocks.

❁ Cut 6 rectangles 1½″ × 3½″ for the Log Cabin blocks.

❁ Cut 6 rectangles 1½″ × 7″ for the Log Cabin blocks.

❁ Cut 6 rectangles 1½″ × 5½″ for the Log Cabin blocks.

❁ Cut 6 rectangles 1½″ × 9″ for the Log Cabin blocks.

❁ Cut 36 squares 2½″ × 2½″ for the checkered border.

Assorted darks
❁ Cut 6 rectangles 1½″ × 2″ for the Log Cabin blocks.

❁ Cut 6 rectangles 1½″ × 5″ for the Log Cabin blocks.

❁ Cut 6 rectangles 1½″ × 3½″ for the Log Cabin blocks.

❁ Cut 6 rectangles 1½″ × 7″ for the Log Cabin blocks.

❁ Cut 6 rectangles 1½″ × 5½″ for the Log Cabin blocks.

❁ Cut 6 rectangles 1½″ × 9″ for the Log Cabin blocks.

❁ Cut 36 squares 2½″ × 2½″ for the checkered border.

LOG CABIN BLOCKS

1. Following the diagrams below, piece together 6 Log Cabin blocks. Press after each strip is added to the block.

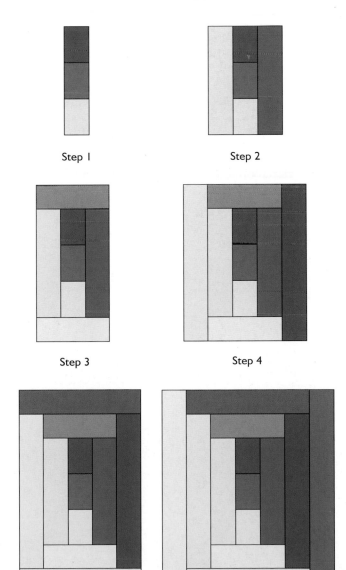

Step 1   Step 2

Step 3   Step 4

Step 5   Step 6

2. Following the diagram below, piece together 2 sets of 3 blocks each. Press.

Make 2.

APPLIQUÉ BLOCK

Cut 1 each of patterns 1–20 (on pullout page). Following the diagram, appliqué the appropriate pieces onto the background.

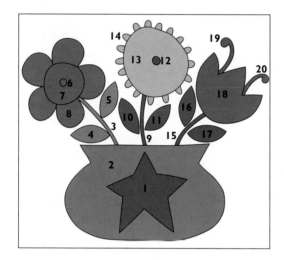

Appliqué block

BORDER

Sew together a row of 9 light and 9 dark squares 2½″ × 2½″. Make 4. Following the diagram, piece together the side borders.

PUTTING IT ALL TOGETHER

1. Following the quilt plan, sew the top and bottom Log Cabin blocks to the appliqué block. Press toward the Log Cabin blocks.

2. Sew the 2 pieced side borders to the quilt top. Press toward the border.

3. Layer the quilt top with batting and backing; baste or pin.

4. Quilt as desired and bind.

Putting it all together

Raggy Flowers
Wall Quilt

I would like to acknowledge and thank Country Threads for its original idea, the raw-edged Bull's-Eye block, which is the basis for the flower in this quilt. You may choose to make your flowers all one color, in which case you will cut fabrics from that color range only, or follow the directions below to make flowers in three different colors. You will have extra blocks that may be used for another wall quilt or the quilt on page 47.

Block Size: 8″ × 16″

Finished Wall Quilt: 35½″ × 27½″

MATERIALS

1¼ yards total of assorted lights for backgrounds

1½ yards total of assorted reds, yellows, and oranges for flowers

¾ yard total of assorted greens for stems, leaves, and border

¼ yard of green for inner border

1¼ yards for backing and binding

½ yard of paper-backed fusible web

CUTTING

Assorted lights

❋ Cut 12 squares 9″ × 9″ for the raggy flower backgrounds.

❋ Cut 12 squares 4½″ × 4½″ for the stem and leaf backgrounds.

Assorted reds, yellows, and oranges

❋ Cut 4 squares 8″ × 8″ from each color for the raggy flowers. Cut a total of 12 squares.

❋ Cut 4 squares 6″ × 6″ from each color for the raggy flowers. Cut a total of 12 squares.

❋ Cut 4 squares 4″ × 4″ from each color for the raggy flowers. Cut a total of 12 squares.

RAGGY FLOWER BLOCKS

1. Fold each of the assorted red, yellow, and orange 8″, 6″, and 4″ squares in quarters and cut a freehand circle.

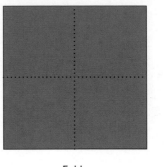

Fold.

Cut.

2. Center a large orange circle on a 9″ background square. Press (this helps keep the circle from shifting). Sew the circle onto the background square, ¼″ from the raw edges. Sew the remaining 3 large orange circles onto different 9″ background squares.

Center circle on square.

3. Turn the blocks over and carefully trim the background fabric within the circle about ¼″ from the stitching line.

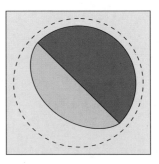

Trim.

4. Center a medium orange circle on top of the large orange circle. Press. Sew around the medium orange circle ¼″ from the raw edges.

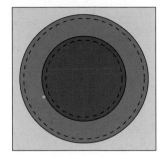

Center circle on square.

5. Sew the remaining 3 medium orange circles onto the remaining large orange circles. Turn the blocks over and carefully trim within the medium orange circles about ¼″ from the stitching line.

6. Center a small orange circle on top of the medium orange circle. Press. Sew around the small orange circle ¼″ from the raw edges.

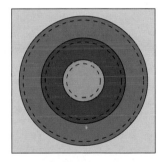

Center circle and sew.

7. Sew the remaining 3 small orange circles onto the remaining medium orange circles. Turn the blocks over and carefully trim within the small circles about ¼″ from the stitching line. Press the blocks.

8. Cut each block into 4 quarters. Each quarter should measure 4½″ square. You will have a total of 16 quarter blocks.

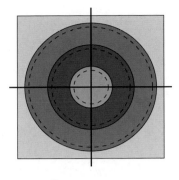

Cut into quarters.

9. Sew 4 different quarter blocks together to form a raggy flower.

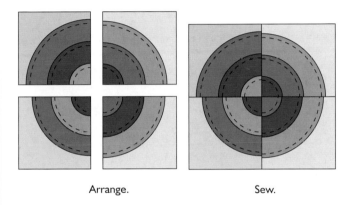

Arrange.   Sew.

10. Repeat Steps 2–9 with the red and yellow circles.

11. To make the stem and leaf blocks, sew 4 different 4½″ light squares together for the background. Press.

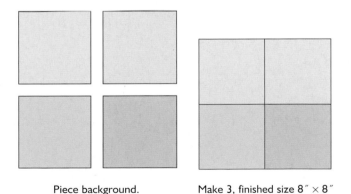

Piece background.   Make 3, finished size 8″ × 8″

12. Referring to the diagram on page 30 and the color photo on page 27, sew a Raggy Flower block to the stem and leaf block.

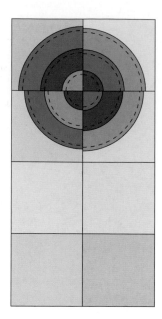

Make 3.

Note: You will have 36 extra quarter blocks to make additional raggy flowers that may be used to make another wall quilt or the quilt on page 47.

APPLIQUÉ

Cut 3 each of patterns 1, 2, and 3. Appliqué stems and leaves onto each block.

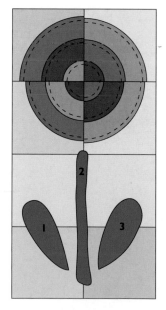

Make 3; finished size 8″ x 16″

Appliqué layout

PUTTING IT ALL TOGETHER

Referring to the quilt plan, sew 3 Raggy Flower blocks together.

Borders

Inner Border

1. Cut 2 strips 2″ × 16½″ for the side borders. Sew to the quilt top and press toward the border.

2. Cut 2 strips 2″ × 27½″ for the top and bottom borders. Sew to the quilt top and press toward the border.

Outer Pieced Border

1. Cut rectangles that vary in length from 2½″ to 5″; cut all at a width of 4½″. Sew pieces together to make 2 strips 4½″ × 19½″ for the side borders. Sew the side borders to the quilt top and press toward the border.

2. Cut rectangles that vary in length from 2½″ to 5″; cut all at a width of 4½″. Sew pieces together to make 2 strips 4½″ × 35½″ for the top and bottom borders. Sew the top and bottom borders to the quilt top and press toward the border.

Finishing

1. Layer the quilt top with batting and backing; baste or pin.

2. Quilt as desired and bind.

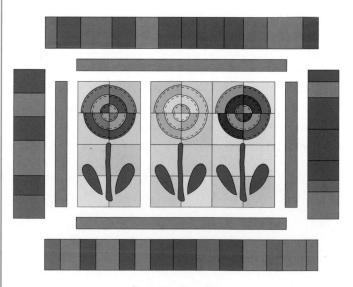

Putting it all together

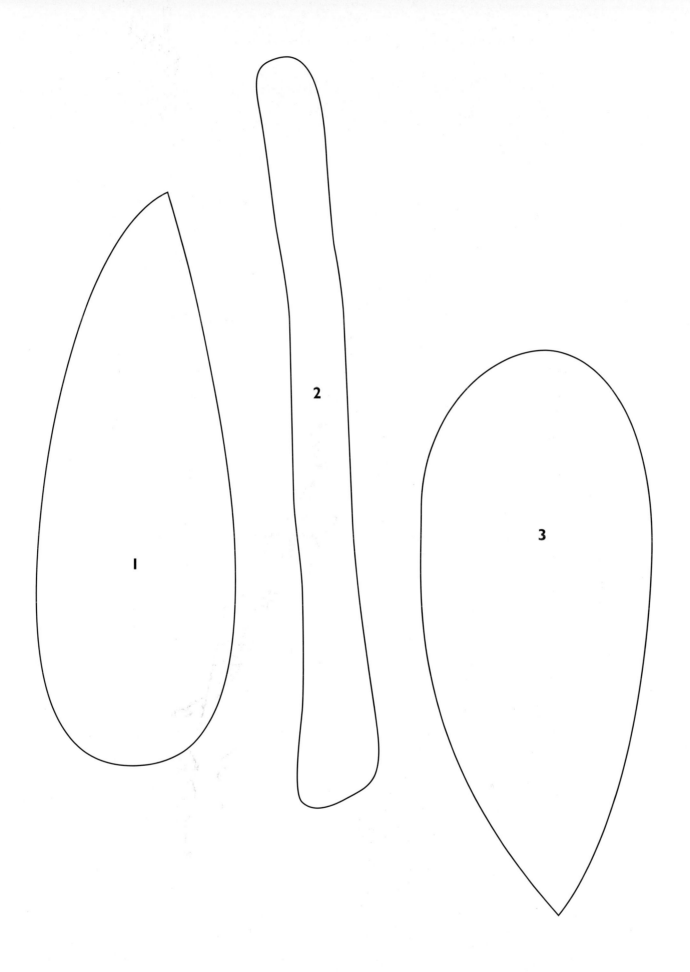

A Bloomin' Dozen
Wall Quilt

F ill your home with the beauty of a summer garden all year round with this *Bloomin' Dozen*. Fresh and new, yet traditional in appeal, this wall quilt blends well with any décor.

Block Size: 7½″ × 10½″

Finished Wall Quilt: 38″ × 59″

MATERIALS

1¾ yards total of assorted lights for backgrounds

1¼ yards total of assorted darks for flowers and pieced border

¾ yard total of assorted greens for leaves and pieced border around appliqué blocks

1¾ yards for backing

⅜ yard for binding

1½ yards of paper-backed fusible web

CUTTING

❀ Cut 12 rectangles 5″ × 8″ from assorted light fabrics for the appliqué block backgrounds.

❀ Cut 327 squares 2″ × 2″ from assorted light fabrics for the pieced border around the appliqué blocks and lattice pieces.

❀ Cut 120 squares 2″ × 2″ from assorted greens for the pieced border around the appliqué blocks.

❀ Cut 116 rectangles 2″ × 5″ from assorted dark fabrics for the pieced border.

APPLIQUÉ BLOCKS

Cut 5 of pattern 1a, cut 5 of pattern 1b, and cut 2 of pattern 1c, reversing the pattern for flower block L. Cut 1 each of all other patterns. Appliqué the appropriate pieces onto each block.

Flower block A; make 1

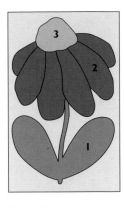

Flower block B; make 1

Flower block C; make 1

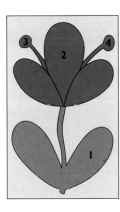

Flower block D; make 1

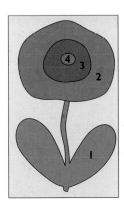

Flower block E; make 1

Flower block F; make 1

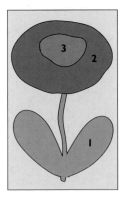

Flower block G; make 1

Flower block H; make 1

Flower block I; make 1

Flower block J; make 1

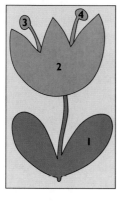

Flower block K; make 1

Flower block L; make 1

PUTTING IT ALL TOGETHER

1. Sew the green and light 2″ squares into rows of 5 squares each.

Make 24.   Make 24.

2. Sew 2 side rows to the flower blocks. Press. Sew the top and bottom rows to the block. Press.

Repeat for appliqué blocks A, C, E, G, I, and K.

3. Sew 2 side rows to the flower blocks. Press. Sew the top and bottom rows to the block.

Repeat for appliqué blocks B, D, F, H, J, and L.

4. Sew 7 light 2″ squares into a row for the vertical lattice pieces. Make 8 sets.

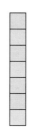

Make 8.

5. Referring to the quilt plan on page 35, sew the lattice pieces to the appliqué flower blocks.

6. Sew 17 light 2″ squares together to form the horizontal lattice pieces. Make 5. Press.

7. Sew 33 light 2″ squares together to form the side lattice pieces. Make 2. Press.

8. Referring to the color photo on page 32, sew the lattice pieces to the quilt. Press toward the lattice.

Pieced Border

1. Sew together 33 rectangles 2″ × 5″ to form the outer side borders.

2. Sew together 25 rectangles 2″ × 5″ to form the outer top and bottom borders.

3. Referring to the diagram on page 35, sew the 2 side borders to the quilt top. Press toward the border. Sew the top and bottom borders. Press toward the border.

Finishing

1. Layer the quilt top with batting and backing; baste or pin.

2. Quilt as desired and bind.

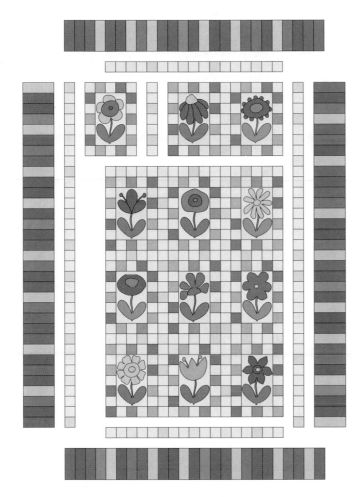

Putting it all together

Alternate Color Option

E

4 3 2

B 3

2

I

3 2

D

4 3

2

A, B, C, H, K

1a

F 3

2

C

2

3

4

1c

F, L

G 3 2

2

H 3

Ib

D, E, G, I, J

Folksy Flower Vases

Wall Quilt

F olk art flower vases are combined with scrappy pieced blocks in this "sophisticated folk" wall quilt. Appliqué borders act as a frame for the quilt. For a more casual look, appliqué backgrounds and borders can be changed from muslin to tans or creams.

Block Size: 10″ × 10″

Finished Wall Quilt: 68½″ × 68½″

MATERIALS

2¾ yards of muslin for appliqué block backgrounds and appliqué border

2½ yards total of assorted darks for pieced blocks, flowers, and border appliqué

¼ yard total of assorted browns for vases

2 yards of green for border and border appliqué

4 yards for backing

⅝ yard for binding

3 yards of paper-backed fusible web

CUTTING

Muslin

✿ Cut 12 squares 6½″ × 6½″ for the appliqué blocks.

✿ Cut 48 squares 2½″ × 2½″ for the appliqué blocks.

✿ Cut 48 squares 2⅞″ × 2⅞″ for the appliqué blocks. Cut the squares on the diagonal to yield 96 triangles.

Assorted dark fabrics

✿ Cut 373 squares 2½″ × 2½″ for the pieced blocks and appliqué blocks.

✿ Cut 48 squares 2⅞″ × 2⅞″ for the appliqué blocks. Cut the squares on the diagonal to yield 96 triangles.

Cut squares on diagonal.

PIECED BLOCKS

1. Sew 5 squares 2½″ × 2½″ in a row.

Make 65.

2. Sew 5 rows together to make the pieced block.

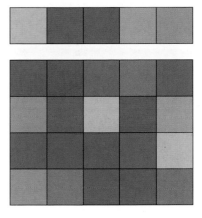

Make 13, finished block 10″ × 10″

APPLIQUÉ BLOCKS

1. Sew the dark triangles to the muslin triangles and press toward the dark fabric.

2. Sew 2 half-square blocks to 1 muslin square in a row.

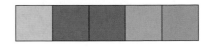

Make 24.

3. Sew the rows to the sides of the 6½″ × 6½″ squares.

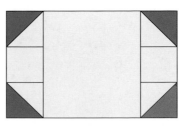

Make 12.

4. Sew 2 half-square blocks to 1 muslin square and 2 dark squares in a row.

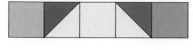

Make 24.

5. Sew the rows to the block center.

Make 12, finished block 10″ × 10″

6. Cut 12 of pattern 1. Cut 2 each of all other patterns. Appliqué the appropriate pieces onto each block.

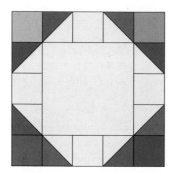

Flower block A; make 2, finished size 10″ × 10″

Flower block B; make 2, finished size 10″ × 10″

Flower block C; make 2, finished size 10″ × 10″

Flower block D; make 2, finished size 10″ × 10″

Flower block E; make 2, finished size 10″ × 10″

Flower block F; make 2, finished size 10″ × 10″

Putting It All Together

Arrange and sew the blocks in 5 rows of 5 blocks each. Sew the rows together. Press.

Borders

Inner Border

1. Piece and cut 2 strips 1½″ × 50½″ from the green fabric for the side borders. Sew to the quilt top and press toward the border.

2. Piece and cut 2 strips 1½″ × 52½″ from the green fabric for the top and bottom borders. Sew to the quilt top and press toward the border.

Appliqué Border

1. Piece and cut 2 strips 7½″ × 52½″ from the muslin for the side borders. Sew to the quilt top. Press.

2. Piece and cut 2 strips 7½″ × 66½″ from the muslin for the top and bottom borders. Sew to the quilt top. Press.

3. Cut 20 each of patterns 1, 2, 3, and 6. Cut 12 of pattern 4. Connect the pattern 5 pieces at the dotted lines. Cut 4 of pattern 5, and cut 4 of pattern 5 reversed.

4. Appliqué the appropriate pieces onto each border.

Outer Border

1. Piece and cut 2 strips 1½″ × 66½″ from the green fabric for the side borders. Sew to the quilt top. Press.

2. Piece and cut 2 strips 1½″ × 68½″ from the green fabric for the top and bottom borders. Sew to the quilt top. Press.

Finishing

1. Layer the quilt top with batting and backing; baste or pin.

2. Quilt as desired and bind.

Putting it all together

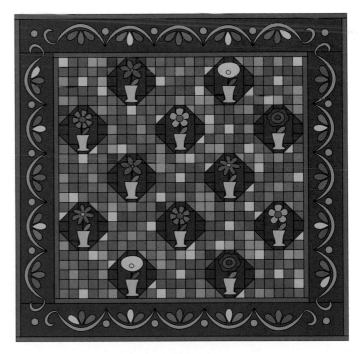

Alternate Color Option

FLOWERING QUILTS

C

4

3

3

B

3

4

3

D

4

3

5

FLOWERING QUILTS

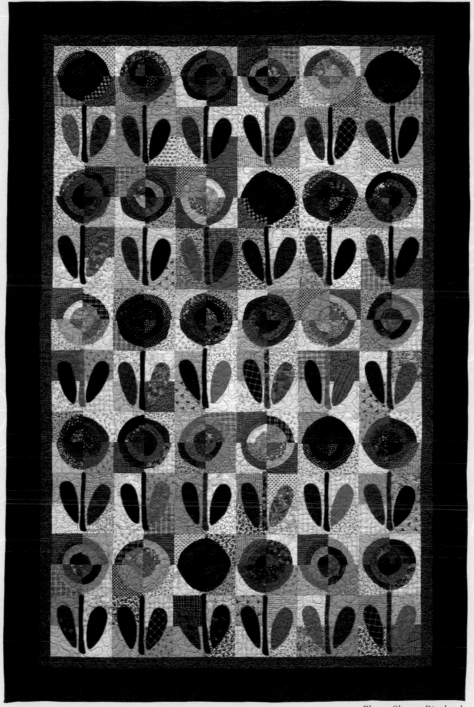

Photo: Sharon Risedorph

Raggy Flowers Lap Quilt

Raw-edged raggy flowers make this quilt bloom with color. The raggy flowers give the quilt a well-loved and worn look.

Block Size: 8″ × 16″

Finished Lap Quilt: 59½″ × 91½″

MATERIALS

4⅓ yards total of assorted lights for backgrounds

5 yards total of assorted yellows, reds, purples, oranges, and pinks for flowers

1½ yards total of assorted greens for stems and leaves

⅝ yard of light green for inner border

1¼ yards of dark green for outer border

6 yards for backing and binding

2½ yards of paper-backed fusible web

CUTTING

Assorted lights

❀ Cut 30 squares 9″ × 9″ for the raggy flower backgrounds.

❀ Cut 120 squares 4½″ × 4½″ for the stem and leaf backgrounds.

Assorted yellows, reds, purples, oranges, and pinks

❀ Cut 6 squares 8″ × 8″ from each color for the raggy flowers. Cut a total of 30 squares.

❀ Cut 6 squares 6″ × 6″ from each color for the raggy flowers. Cut a total of 30 squares.

❀ Cut 4 squares 4″ × 4″ from each color for the raggy flowers. Cut a total of 30 squares.

RAGGY FLOWER BLOCKS

To make the Raggy Flower blocks, follow the directions from the *Raggy Flower Wall Quilt* on pages 28–30. Make a total of 30 Raggy Flower blocks: 6 each of the assorted reds, purples, oranges, pinks, and yellows. Appliqué pattern templates for the stems and leaves are on page 31. Cut 30 each of patterns 1, 2, and 3.

PUTTING IT ALL TOGETHER

Arrange and sew the Raggy Flower blocks in 5 rows of 6 blocks each. See the diagram on page 49.

Borders

Inner Border

1. Piece and cut 2 strips 2″ × 80½″ for the side borders. Sew to the quilt top and press toward the border.

2. Piece and cut 2 strips 2″ × 51½″ for the top and bottom borders. Sew to the quilt top and press toward the border.

Outer Border

1. Piece and cut 2 strips 4½″ × 83½″ for the side borders. Sew to the quilt top and press toward the border.

2. Piece and cut 2 strips 4½″ × 59½″ for the top and bottom borders. Sew to the quilt top and press toward the border.

Finishing

1. Layer the quilt top with batting and backing; baste or pin.

2. Quilt as desired and bind.

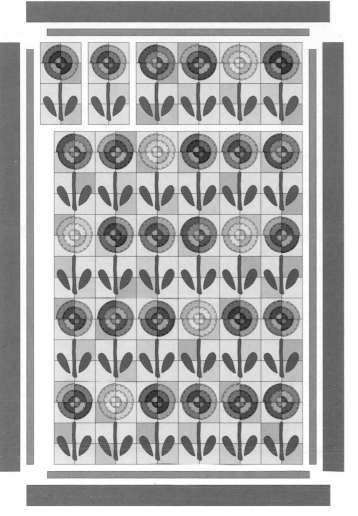

Putting it all together

Alternate Color Option

Photo: Sharon Risedorph

Stripes and Flower Vines
✳ Lap Quilt

Randomly pieced stripes offset folksy appliqué flower vines for a simple yet sophisticated look. Shades of black and gray lend an old-fashioned feeling to this quilt.

Block Size: 9″ × 9″

Finished Lap Quilt: 59½″ × 90½″

MATERIALS

2¾ yards of gray for appliqué flower backgrounds

4 yards total of assorted blacks, prints, plaids, and checks for pieced blocks

¾ yard total of assorted reds for flowers

⅛ yard of black for flower centers

¾ yard total of assorted tans for stems and leaves

6 yards for backing and binding

2 yards of paper-backed fusible web

CUTTING

❁ Cut 1 piece 9½″ × 90½″ from gray for the center appliqué background.

❁ Cut 2 pieces 7½″ × 90½″ from gray for the side appliqué backgrounds.

Assorted black prints, plaids, and checks

❁ Cut 80 rectangles 1¾″ × 9½″ for the pieced blocks.

❁ Cut 80 rectangles 1¼″ × 9½″ for the pieced blocks.

❁ Cut 40 rectangles 2½″ × 9½″ for the pieced blocks.

❁ Cut 40 rectangles 1″ × 9½″ for the pieced blocks.

❁ Cut 40 rectangles 2″ × 9½″ for the pieced blocks.

❁ Cut 40 rectangles 1½″ × 9½″ for the pieced blocks.

To keep the rectangles organized, separate them according to width and place them in separately marked containers. To make the pieced blocks, you will be using 2 rectangles 1¾″ × 9½″ and 2 rectangles 1¼″ × 9½″ and 1 each of the other sizes per block.

PIECED BLOCKS

1. Sew the following rectangles together in random order to make a pieced block:

1″ × 9½″ rectangle (1)	1¾″ × 9½″ rectangles (2)
1¼″ × 9½″ rectangles (2)	2″ × 9½″ rectangle (1)
1½″ × 9½″ rectangle (1)	2½″ × 9½″ rectangle (1)

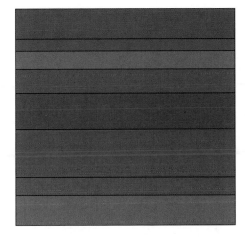

Make 40, finished size 9″ × 9″

The blocks will be different because they are sewn in random order, but all will measure 9½″ × 9½″. Refer to the diagram on page 53.

2. Sew the blocks together in 4 rows of 10 blocks each. Press flat. Refer to the diagram on page 53.

APPLIQUÉ

Cut 1 each of patterns 1 and 6, cut 13 of pattern 2, cut 14 of pattern 3, and cut 2 each of patterns 4 and 5. Cut 15 each of patterns 7 and 8, and cut 30 each of patterns 9, 10, and 11. Referring to the diagrams, appliqué the appropriate pieces onto the pieces.

Make 2.

Make 1.

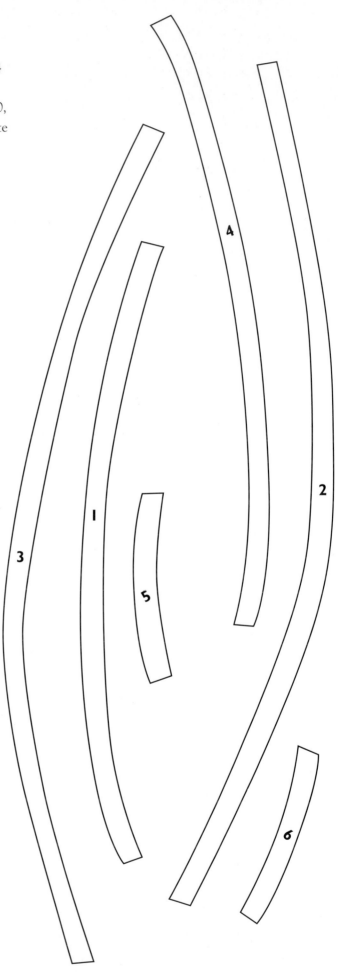

PUTTING IT ALL TOGETHER

1. Referring to the quilt plan, sew strips together, alternating pieced block rows and appliqué pieces. Press flat.

2. Layer the quilt top with batting and backing; baste or pin.

3. Quilt as desired and bind.

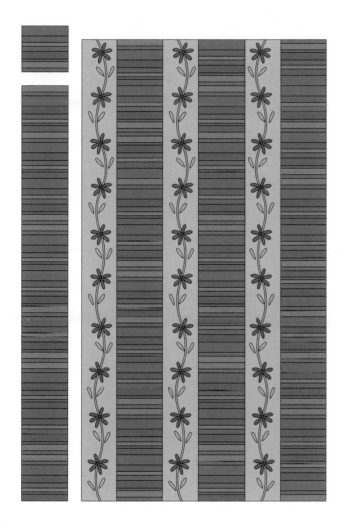

Putting it all together

Alternate Color Option

FLOWERING QUILTS

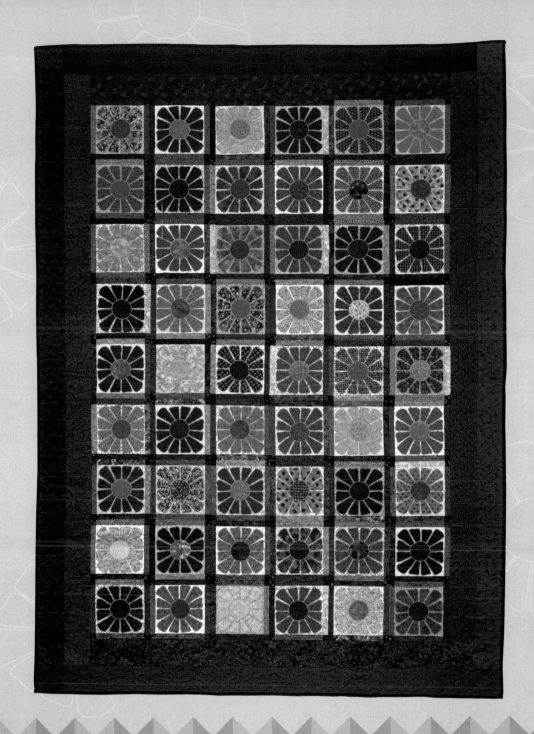

Square Flowers
Lap Quilt

Remember the splendor of your garden throughout the year when you stitch these vibrant, stylized square flowers.

Block Size: 8″ × 8″

Finished Lap Quilt: 62½″ × 86½″

MATERIALS

2½ yards total of assorted lights for background squares

2¼ yards total of assorted reds, purples, pinks, yellows, blues, and oranges for flowers

3½ yards total of assorted greens for lattice pieces and border

⅜ yard total of assorted blacks for corner squares

5½ yards for backing and binding

5¼ yards of paper-backed fusible web

CUTTING

✿ Cut 54 squares 7″ × 7″ from assorted lights for the appliqué backgrounds.

✿ Cut 216 rectangles 7″ × 1¼″ from assorted greens for the lattice pieces.

✿ Cut 216 squares 1¼″ × 1¼″ from assorted blacks for the corner squares.

APPLIQUÉ BLOCKS

1. Cut 54 each of patterns 1 and 2. Appliqué the appropriate pieces onto the blocks.

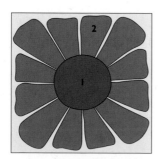

Make 54.

2. Sew a 1¼″ square to each end of a 7″ × 1¼″ rectangle. Press.

Make 108.

3. Sew 2 side lattice pieces to an appliqué block. Press toward the lattice.

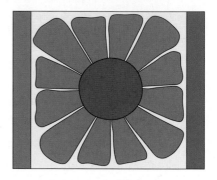

Sew lattice pieces to sides of appliqué block.

4. Sew the top and bottom lattice pieces to the appliqué block. Press.

Make 54; finished size 8″ x 8″

PUTTING IT ALL TOGETHER

Referring to the quilt plan, arrange and sew the blocks together in 9 rows of 6 blocks each. Press.

Border

1. From the assorted green fabrics, piece and cut the following border strips:

$4'' \times 48\frac{1}{2}''$ for border 1

$4'' \times 76''$ for border 2

$4'' \times 52''$ for border 3

$4'' \times 79\frac{1}{2}''$ for border 4

$4'' \times 55\frac{1}{2}''$ for border 5

$4'' \times 83''$ for border 6

$4'' \times 59''$ for border 7

$4'' \times 86\frac{1}{2}''$ for border 8

2. Following the border sequence diagram below, sew the borders onto the quilt top, clockwise, pressing toward the border after each addition.

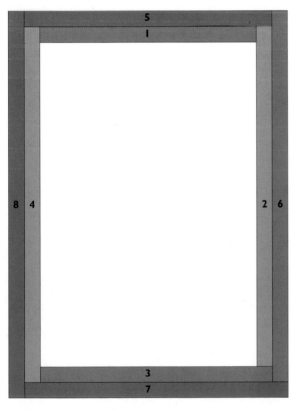

Border sequence

Finishing

1. Layer the quilt with batting and backing; baste or pin.

2. Quilt as desired and bind.

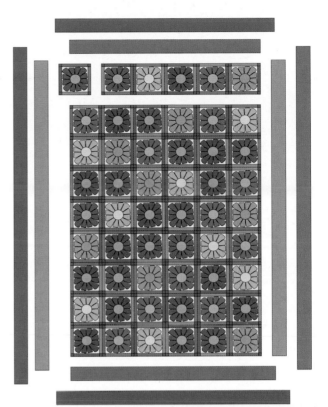

Putting it all together

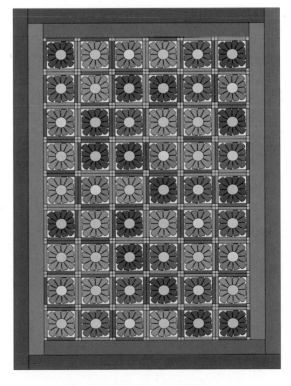

Alternate Color Option

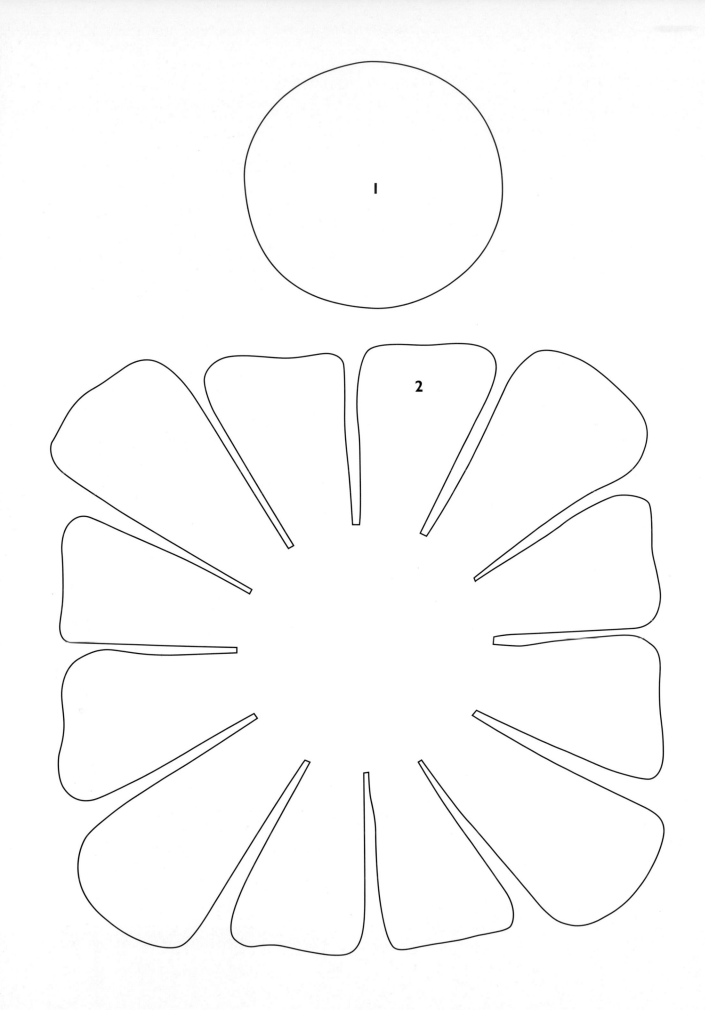

Red-Eyed Blooms
Lap Quilt

Large, bold appliqué flowers make this quilt bloom with color. A scrapper's delight—even a 2½″ piece can debut in this quilt. The wide variety of scraps adds visual pleasure to this free-spirited folk art quilt.

Block Size: 10″ × 10″

Finished Lap Quilt: 62½″ × 72½″

MATERIALS

3⅜ yards total of assorted lights for backgrounds

2½ yards total of assorted yellows, golds, purples, light blues, dark blues, navy blues, oranges, and rusts for flowers

1 yard total of assorted reds for flowers and centers

1¾ yards total of assorted greens for pieced border and pieced blocks

¾ yard of tan for inner pieced border

4¾ yards for backing and binding

6 yards of paper-backed fusible web

CUTTING

❋ Cut 630 squares 2½″ × 2½″ from assorted lights for the pieced backgrounds.

❋ Cut 60 squares 2⅞″ × 2⅞″ from assorted lights for the pieced backgrounds. Cut the squares on the diagonal for a total of 120 triangles.

Cut squares on diagonal.

❋ Cut 84 squares 2⅞″ × 2⅞″ from assorted greens for the pieced backgrounds and pieced border. Cut the squares on the diagonal for a total of 168 triangles.

❋ Cut 22 rectangles 6½″ × 2½″ from tan fabric for the inner pieced border.

❋ Cut 24 squares 2⅞″ × 2⅞″ from tan fabric. Cut the squares on the diagonal for a total of 48 triangles.

PIECED BACKGROUNDS

1. Sew together 5 squares 2½″ × 2½″ to form a row. Press.

Make 90.

2. Sew together 3 squares 2½″ × 2½″ to form a row. Press.

Make 60.

3. Sew 120 assorted light triangles to 120 assorted green triangles. Press toward the green triangle.

Make 120.

4. Sew the half-square triangle blocks to each of the rows containing 3 squares. Press.

Make 60.

5. Sew the rows together to form the pieced blocks.

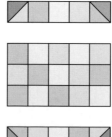 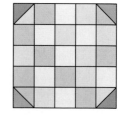

Pieced block assembly

Make 30.

APPLIQUÉ BLOCKS

Cut 30 each of patterns 1 and 2; cut 120 each of patterns 3 and 4. Appliqué the appropriate pieces onto the blocks. Make each block unique by varying the way the petals overlap each other and turning the center different directions.

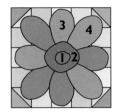

Make 30; finished size 10″ x 10″

PUTTING IT ALL TOGETHER

Referring to the quilt plan, arrange and sew the blocks together in 6 rows of 5 blocks each. Sew the rows together. Press.

Borders

Inner Border

1. For the inner pieced border, sew 48 tan triangles to 48 assorted green triangles on the diagonal. Press. Sew to the ends of the tan rectangles. Referring to the diagram, piece the 2 side borders. Sew the side borders to the quilt top and press toward the border.

2. Referring to the quilt plan, piece the top and bottom borders. Press. Sew the top and bottom borders to the quilt top and press toward the border.

Outer Border

1. Cut rectangles that vary in length from 2½″ to 5″; cut all at a width of 4½″. Sew the pieces together to make 2 strips 4½″ × 54½″ for the top and bottom borders. Sew the top and bottom borders to the quilt top and press toward the border.

2. Cut rectangles that vary in length from 2½″ to 5″; cut all at a width of 4½″. Sew the pieces together to make 2 strips 4½″ × 72½″ for the side borders. Sew the side borders to the quilt top and press toward the border.

Finishing

1. Layer the quilt top with batting and backing; baste or pin.

2. Quilt as desired and bind.

Putting it all together

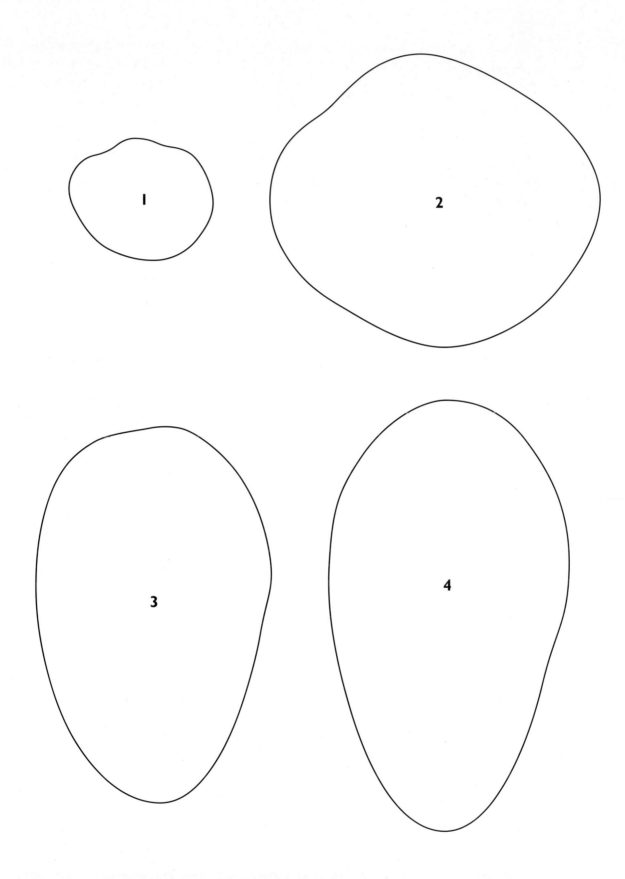

FLOWERING QUILTS

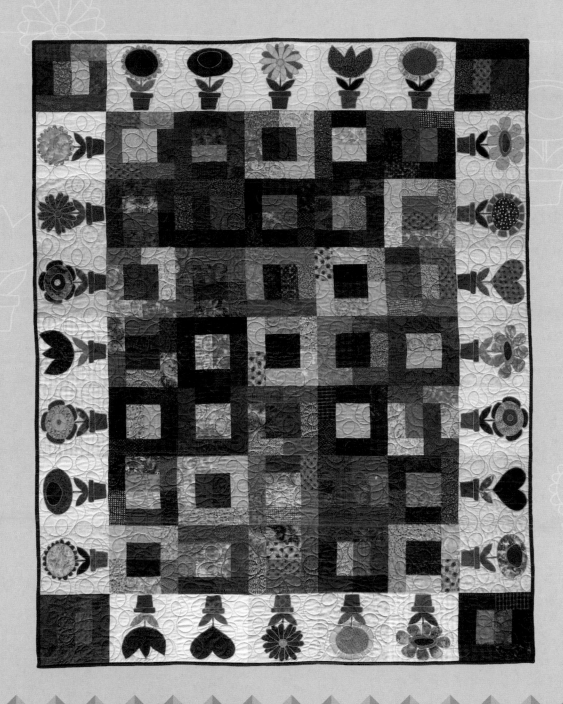

Garden Path
Lap Quilt

This lap quilt features a potted flower border set off by vibrant pieced blocks. Contrast in color within the blocks is the key to success with these pieced blocks. You may also achieve this contrast by alternating lights and darks within the blocks for a different look.

Block Size: 8″ × 8″

Finished Lap Quilt:: 56½″ × 72½″

MATERIALS

1¾ yards total of assorted lights for appliqué block backgrounds

2¼ yards total of assorted reds, purples, and pinks for pieced blocks and appliqué flowers

1 yard total of assorted yellows and golds for pieced blocks and appliqué flowers

1 yard total of assorted oranges and rusts for pieced blocks and appliqué flowers and pots

1 yard total of assorted greens for pieced blocks and appliqué stems and leaves

4¾ yards for backing and binding

4 yards of paper-backed fusible web

CUTTING

❀ Cut 24 squares 8½″ × 8½″ from assorted lights for the appliqué block backgrounds.

❀ For the pieced blocks you will need a total of 312 rectangles 2½″ × 4½″. To make the quilt as shown, cut the following:

Cut 50 rectangles 2½″ × 4½″ from assorted reds.

Cut 60 rectangles 2½″ × 4½″ from assorted purples.

Cut 36 rectangles 2½″ × 4½″ from assorted pinks.

Cut 66 rectangles 2½″ × 4½″ from assorted yellows and golds.

❀ Cut 40 rectangles 2½″ × 4½″ from assorted oranges and rusts.

❀ Cut 60 rectangles 2½″ × 4½″ from assorted greens.

PIECED BLOCKS

Following the diagrams below, sew 8 rectangles together to make a pieced block. Make 39 pieced blocks.

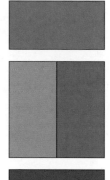

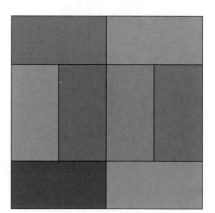

Make 39, finished size 8″ × 8″

APPLIQUÉ BLOCKS

Cut 24 each of patterns 1 and 2. Cut 3 each of all the other patterns. Appliqué the appropriate pieces onto each block.

Block A; make 3, finished size 8″ × 8″

Block D; make 3, finished size 8″ × 8″

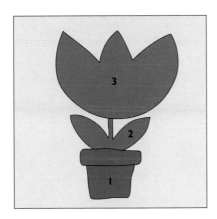

Block B; make 3, finished size 8″ × 8″

Block E; make 3, finished size 8″ × 8″

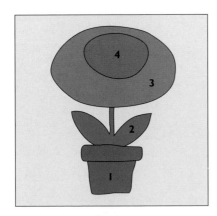

Block C; make 3, finished size 8″ × 8″

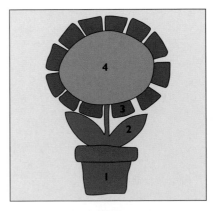

Block F; make 3, finished size 8″ × 8″

Block G; make 3, finished size 8″ × 8″

Block H; make 3, finished size 8″ × 8″

PUTTING IT ALL TOGETHER

Arrange and sew the pieced blocks in 7 rows of 5 blocks each. Referring to the quilt plan, sew the rows together to form the pieced block section of the quilt top. Press.

Border

1. Referring to the quilt plan, sew 2 rows of 5 appliqué blocks together for the top and bottom borders. Add a pieced block on each end of the appliqué block row. Press.

2. Referring to the quilt plan, sew 2 rows of 7 appliqué blocks together for the side borders. Press.

3. Sew the side borders to the quilt top. Press toward the border. Sew the top and bottom borders to the quilt top. Press toward the border.

Finishing

1. Layer the quilt top with batting and backing; baste or pin.

2. Quilt as desired and bind.

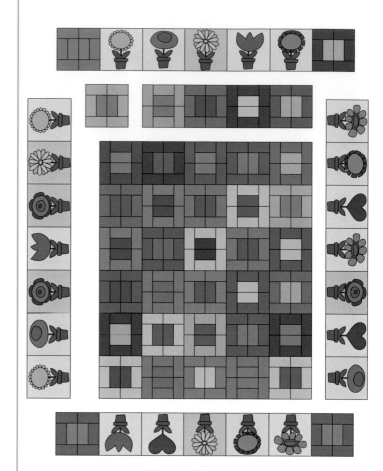

Putting it all together

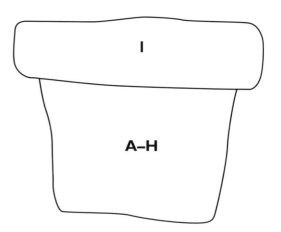

H

4

6 5

3

E

4

3

3

A

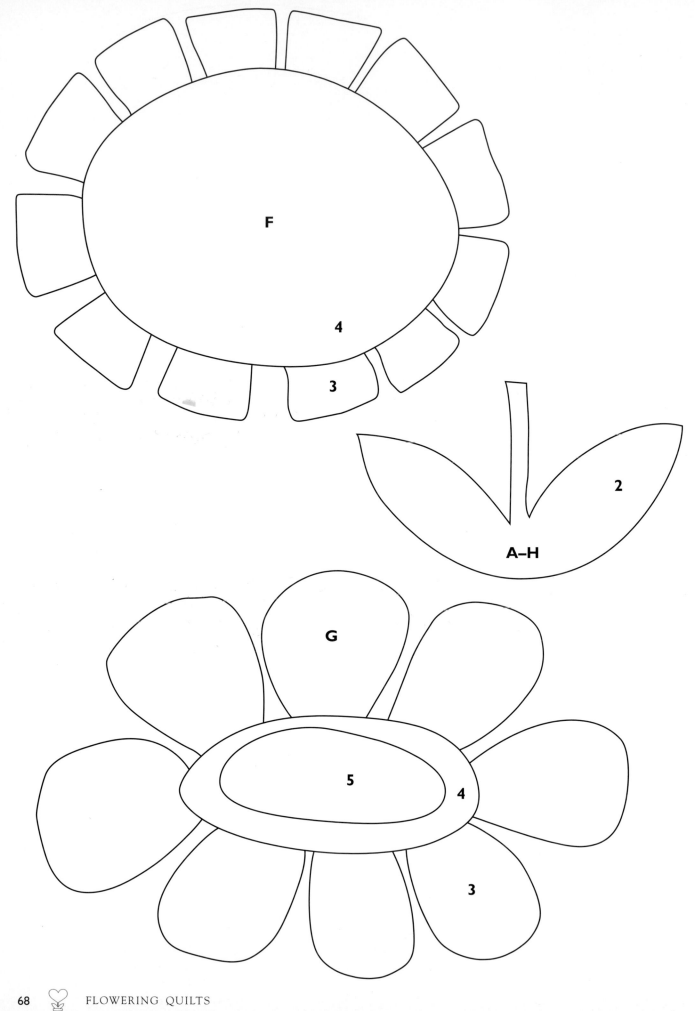

F

4

3

2

A–H

G

5

4

3

4

3

C

D

6

5

4

3

3

B

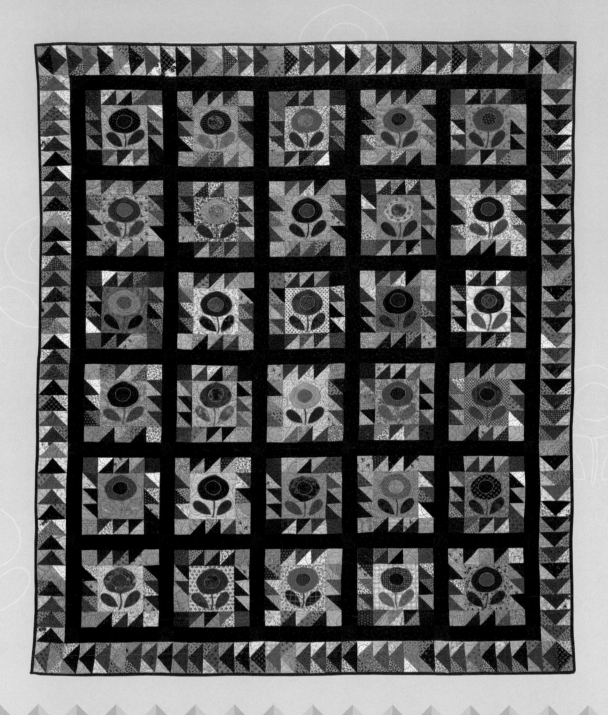

Pocketful of Posies
Quilt

S ingle appliqué flowers are framed by scrappy pieced blocks. This quilt was designed to be a scrapper's heaven. The quilt top is made entirely from scraps, with the exception of the lattice strips. A Flying Geese border offers yet another chance to make great use of your stash.

Block Size: 10″ × 10″

Finished Quilt: 70½″ × 82½″

MATERIALS

1⅛ yards total of assorted lights for appliqué backgrounds

2½ yards total of assorted lights for pieced blocks and pieced border

2¾ yards total of assorted darks for pieced blocks and pieced border

1¼ yards total of assorted blues, yellows, oranges, reds, and purples for flowers

½ yard total of assorted greens for stems and leaves

⅜ yard of red for lattice squares

1⅞ yards of brown for lattice pieces

5 yards for backing

⅝ yard for binding

2½ yards of paper-backed fusible web

CUTTING

Assorted lights

❀ Cut 30 squares 6½″ × 6½″ for the appliqué backgrounds.

❀ Cut 60 squares 2½″ × 2½″ for the pieced blocks.

❀ Cut 180 squares 2⅞″ × 2⅞″ for the pieced blocks. Cut the squares on the diagonal for a total of 360 triangles.

❀ Cut 144 squares 2⅞″ × 2⅞″ for the pieced border. Cut the squares on the diagonal for a total of 288 triangles.

Assorted darks

❀ Cut 60 squares 2½″ ¥ 2½″ for the pieced blocks.

❀ Cut 180 squares 2⅞″ × 2⅞″ for the pieced blocks. Cut the squares on the diagonal for a total of 360 triangles.

❀ Cut 36 squares 5¼″ × 5¼″ for the pieced border. Cut the squares on the diagonal twice from corner to corner for a total of 144 triangles.

Cut diagonally twice from corner to corner.

❀ Cut 71 rectangles 2½″ × 10½″ from brown fabric for the lattice pieces.

❀ Cut 42 squares 2½″ × 2½″ from red fabric for the lattice squares.

APPLIQUÉ

Cut 30 each of patterns 1, 2, 3, 4, and 5. Appliqué the appropriate pieces onto each block.

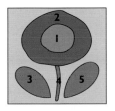

Make 30.

PIECED BLOCKS

1. Sew 360 light triangles to 360 dark triangles on the diagonal edge to make 360 blocks. Press.

Make 360.

2. Sew 3 half-square blocks to form a row.

Make 60.

3. Sew 30 rows to the sides of the appliqué background squares. Sew 4 dark squares to the ends of 2 rows of triangles. Make 30. Sew to the top and bottom of the background square. Make sure the dark triangles face the center square. Press.

Make 15, finished size 10″ × 10″

4. Sew 3 half-square blocks to form a row.

Make 60.

5. Sew 30 rows to the sides of the appliqué background squares. Sew 4 light squares to the ends of 2 rows of triangles. Make 30. Sew to the top and bottom of the background square. Make sure the light triangles face the center square. Press.

Make 15, finished size 10″ × 10″

PUTTING IT ALL TOGETHER

1. Arrange the pieced blocks in 6 rows of 5 blocks each, alternating light and dark blocks. Sew 2½″ × 10½″ brown lattice pieces to the pieced blocks to form rows. See the diagram on page 73.

2. Referring to the quilt plan on page 73, piece the horizontal lattice pieces. Make 7. Sew the horizontal lattice pieces to the rows. Press.

Flying Geese Border

1. Sew 2 light triangles to 1 dark triangle on the diagonal edges.

Sew the triangles.

Make 144, finished size 2″ × 4″

2. Arrange and sew 2 rows of 37 Flying Geese units together for the side borders. Press.

3. Arrange and sew 2 rows of 31 Flying Geese units together for the top and bottom borders.

4. Arrange and sew 8 Flying Geese units for the corner units.

5. Sew the corner units to each end of the top and bottom borders. Press.

6. Sew the side borders to the quilt top. Press. Sew the top and bottom borders to the quilt top. Press.

Finishing

1. Layer the quilt top with batting and backing; baste or pin.

2. Quilt as desired and bind.

Putting it all together

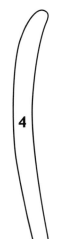

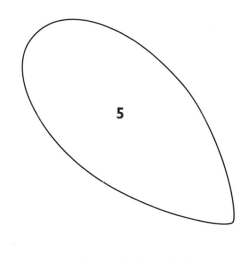

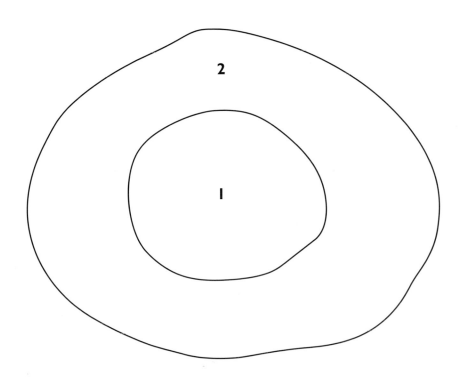

Photo: Sharon Risedorph

Red Posies  Quilt

An appliqué border of red posies surrounds the traditional, and very easily pieced, Rail Fence variation that makes up the body of the quilt top. The combination gives the quilt a look of folksy elegance.

Block Size: 6″ × 6″

Finished Quilt: 89½″ × 101½″

MATERIALS

⅛ yard or scraps of brown for Block A

⅛ yard or scraps of light for Block A

⅜ yard of dark gold for Block B

⅝ yard of light gold for Block B

¼ yard of medium green for Block C

⅓ yard of green plaid for Block C

¼ yard of light for Block D

⅜ yard of brown for Block D

⅓ yard of light green for Block E

½ yard of black textured solid for Block E

⅜ yard of red for Block F

⅝ yard of dark red for Block F

⅜ yard of dark green for Block G

⅝ yard of green for Block G

⅜ yard of olive green for Block H

⅝ yard of dark brown textured solid for Block H

¼ yard of green for Block I

⅜ yard of dark for Block I

¼ yard of red for Block J

⅓ yard of brown for Block J

½ yard total of assorted reds for flowers

¼ yard of black plaid for flower centers

¾ yard total of assorted greens for leaves

1½ yards of black for vines

1 yard of black for inner and outer border

1½ yards of tan (Fabric A) for appliqué border

1½ yards of cream (Fabric B) for appliqué border

8¾ yards for backing

¾ yard for binding

4 yards of paper-backed fusible web

CUTTING

Tip Some of the blocks may be strip pieced. To piece using this method, you will cut 3 strips 2½″ × the width of the fabric (usually 40″–42″). Sew the strips together along the length. Press. Cut at 6½″ intervals. You will get 6 blocks from each set of strips.

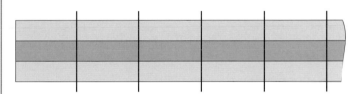

Cut strips at 6½″ intervals.

✿ Cut 1 rectangle 2½″ × 6½″ from brown for Block A.

✿ Cut 2 rectangles 2½″ × 6½″ from light for Block A.

✿ Cut 20 rectangles 2½″ × 6½″ from dark gold for Block B.

✿ Cut 40 rectangles 2½″ × 6½″ from light gold for Block B.

✿ Cut 8 rectangles 2½″ × 6½″ from medium green for Block C.

✿ Cut 16 rectangles 2½″ × 6½″ from green plaid for Block C.

✿ Cut 12 rectangles 2½″ × 6½″ from light for Block D.

✿ Cut 24 rectangles 2½″ × 6½″ from brown for Block D.

✿ Cut 16 rectangles 2½″ × 6½″ from light green for Block E.

- Cut 32 rectangles 2½″ × 6½″ from black textured solid for Block E.
- Cut 24 rectangles 2½″ × 6½″ from red for Block F.
- Cut 48 rectangles 2½″ × 6½″ from dark red for Block F.
- Cut 22 rectangles 2½″ × 6½″ from dark green for Block G.
- Cut 44 rectangles 2½″ × 6½″ from green for Block G.
- Cut 20 rectangles 2½″ × 6½″ from olive green for Block H.
- Cut 40 rectangles 2½″ × 6½″ from dark brown textured solid for Block H.
- Cut 12 rectangles 2½″ × 6½″ from green for Block I.
- Cut 24 rectangles 2½″ × 6½″ from dark for Block I.
- Cut 8 rectangles 2½″ × 6½″ from red for Block J.
- Cut 16 rectangles 2½″ × 6½″ from brown for Block J.

If you are piecing blocks from scraps, you will need a total of 429 rectangles 2½″ × 6½″.

PIECED BLOCKS

Referring to the diagrams, piece the blocks. Make a total of 143 blocks.

Block A; make 1,
finished size 6″ × 6″

Block B; make 20,
finished size 6″ × 6″

Block C; make 8,
finished size 6″ × 6″

Block D; make 12,
finished size 6″ × 6″

Block E; make 16,
finished size 6″ × 6″

Block F; make 24,
finished size 6″ × 6″

Block G; make 22,
finished size 6″ × 6″

Block H; make 20,
finished size 6″ × 6″

Block I; make 12,
finished size 6″ × 6″

Block J; make 8,
finished size 6″ × 6″

PUTTING IT ALL TOGETHER

Arrange and piece the blocks together in 13 rows of 11 blocks each. Refer to the diagram on page 78.

Borders

Inner Border

1. Piece and cut 2 strips 1½″ × 78½″ for the sides. Sew to the quilt top and press toward the border.

2. Piece and cut 2 strips 1½″ × 68½″ for the top and bottom. Sew to the quilt top and press toward the border.

Appliqué Border

1. Piece and cut 2 strips each from tan (Fabric A) and cream (Fabric B) 10″ × 40½″ for the side borders. Piece on the short ends. Press.

2. Cut 4 each of patterns 1–24 (on pullout page), reversing 2 of each. Appliqué the appropriate pieces to the side borders. Press from the wrong side.

3. Sew the side borders to the quilt top. Press toward the border.

4. Piece and cut 2 strips each from tan (Fabric A) and cream (Fabric B) 10″ × 44″ for the top and bottom borders. Piece on the short ends. Press.

5. Cut 4 each of patterns 25–49 (on pullout page), reversing 2 of each. Appliqué the appropriate pieces to the top and bottom borders. Press from the wrong side.

6. Sew the top and bottom borders to the quilt top and press toward the border.

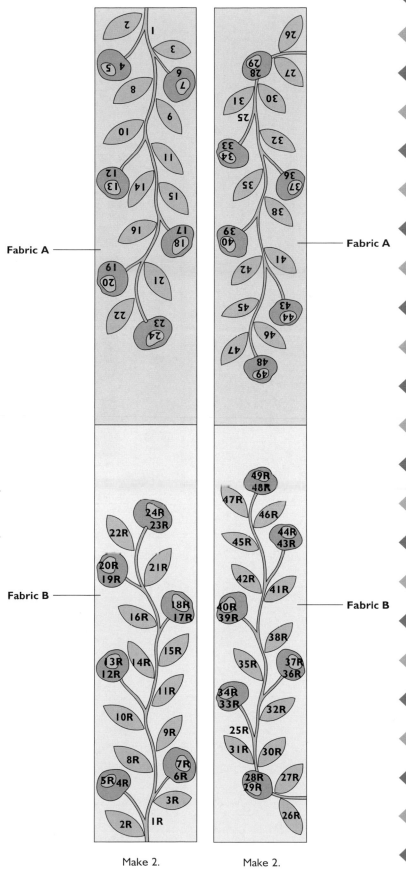

Fabric A

Fabric A

Fabric B

Fabric B

Make 2.   Make 2.

Outer Border

1. Piece and cut 2 strips 1½″ × 99½″ for the side borders. Sew to the quilt top and press toward the border.

2. Piece and cut 2 strips 1½″ × 89½″ for the top and bottom borders. Sew to the quilt top and press toward the border.

Finishing

1. Layer the quilt with batting and backing; baste or pin.

2. Quilt as desired and bind.

Putting it all together

Alternate Color Option

Mortensen Photography

About the Author

Kim Schaefer is from southeastern Wisconsin, where she lives with her husband, Gary, and sons, Max, Ben, Sam, and Gator, and dog, Rio—all of whom she lovingly refers to as the "Neanderthals." Kim and Gary also have two daughters, Cody and Ali. Cody lives nearby, and Ali attends college in Minnesota. Kim's stepsons, Gary Jr. and Dax, also live nearby, and her stepdaughters, Tina and Danielle, live in Phoenix.

Kim began sewing at an early age, which, according to Kim, was a nightmare for her mom, who continually and patiently untangled bobbin messes. Kim was formally educated at the University of Wisconsin in Milwaukee, where she studied fine arts and majored in fibers.

At age 23, Kim took her first quilting class and was immediately hooked.

In 1996, Little Country Quilts was born and made its debut at Quilt Market in Minneapolis. In addition to designing quilt patterns, Kim designs fabric for Andover/Makower and works with Leo Licensing, which licenses her designs for nonfabric products.

▶ **FOR MORE INFORMATION**

Ask for a free catalog:

C&T Publishing, Inc.

P.O. Box 1456

Lafayette, CA 94549

800-284-1114

email: ctinfo@ctpub.com

website: www.ctpub.com

▶ **QUILTING SUPPLIES**

Cotton Patch Mail Order

3404 Hall Lane

Dept. CTB

Lafayette, CA 94549

800-835-4418   925-283-7883

email: quiltusa@yahoo.com

website: www.quiltusa.com

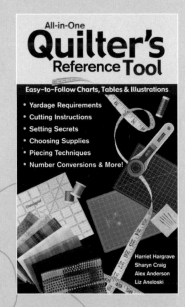
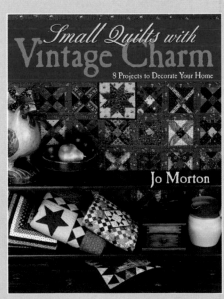